Taylor Swift Biography For Kids

Inspirational Journey From Country Girl to
Pop Princess, Finding Her Voice, Navigating
Fame, and Trailblazing in the Music
Industry For little Dreamers

Academic Press

Table of Contents

Introduction

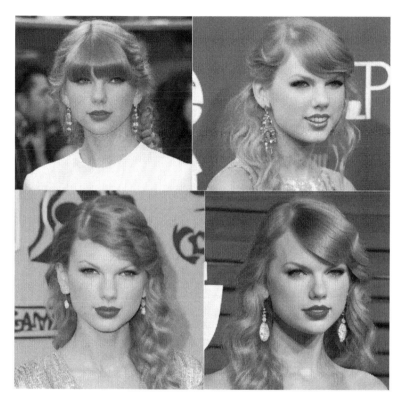

Have you ever dreamed of becoming a superstar? Of singing your heart out on a stage, surrounded by millions of fans who adore you? Of writing songs that touch people's lives and make them feel less alone?

If you have, then you might have something in common with Taylor Swift. She is one of the most famous and successful singers in the world, but she didn't start out that way. She was once a young girl who loved music and stories, who had big dreams and faced many challenges.

In this book, you will discover how Taylor Swift went from a country girl to a pop princess, and how she never gave up on her passion. You will learn about her struggles and triumphs, her joys and sorrows, her failures and achievements. You will see how she used her talent, creativity, and courage to overcome obstacles and reach her goals. You will also find out how she inspires others to follow their dreams and be themselves.

Taylor Swift's story is not just about fame and fortune. It is about resilience and determination, about love and kindness, about finding your voice and expressing yourself. It is a story that will make you laugh, cry, and cheer. It is a story that will inspire you to be fearless.

Are you ready to embark on this journey with Taylor Swift? Then turn the page and let the adventure begin!

Chapter 1: A Star is Born

- "Early life and family dynamics.

Taylor Swift was born on December 13, 1989, in West Reading, Pennsylvania, to Scott and Andrea Swift. She had a younger brother, Austin, who shared her love for music and stories. Taylor grew up on a Christmas tree farm that her father had bought from one of his clients. She loved riding horses and playing with her pony, Ginger. She also enjoyed reading books and writing poems, and showed a talent for both at an early age. She won a national poetry contest when she was in fourth grade with a poem called "Monster in My Closet".

Taylor's passion for music was sparked by her grandmother, Marjorie Finlay, who was a professional opera singer. Taylor would listen to her grandmother's recordings and sing along with her. She also admired country artists like Shania Twain and the Dixie Chicks, who inspired her to write her own songs. She learned to play the guitar when she was 12, after a computer repairman taught her a few chords. She wrote her first song, "Lucky You", about a girl who moved away and missed her friends.

Taylor's family was very supportive of her musical aspirations. They often drove her to Nashville, Tennessee, where she performed at open mic nights and songwriters' showcases. They also helped her find a manager, Dan Dymtrow, who got her a deal with Sony/ATV as the youngest songwriter ever signed by the company. Taylor's parents also made a big sacrifice for her career: they moved to Hendersonville, Tennessee, when she was 14, so she could be closer to the music industry.

Taylor faced some challenges and setbacks in her early years as well. She was bullied at school for being different and for pursuing her dreams. She also had to deal with rejection and criticism from some record labels, who wanted her to change her style or sing other people's songs. She refused to compromise her vision and stayed true to herself. She eventually found a label that believed in her, Big Machine Records, and released her debut album, Taylor Swift, in 2006.

Taylor Swift's early life and family dynamics shaped her identity and aspirations as a singer-songwriter. She learned to be resilient, determined, creative, and courageous from her experiences and from her loved ones. She also developed a strong sense of gratitude and generosity, as she always remembered where she came from and how far she had come. She used her music as a way to express herself and to connect with others. She also used it as a way to inspire young people to follow their dreams and to be fearless.

- Unveiling Taylor's passion for music.

Music has always been a part of Taylor Swift's life. She was born with a natural gift for melody and rhythm, and a curiosity for sounds and stories. She was fascinated by the songs she heard on the radio, the tunes her grandmother sang, and the instruments she saw in her home. She wanted to learn how to make music of her own, and how to share it with others.

Taylor's musical journey began when she was a toddler, and her parents gave her a toy piano. She would play with it for hours, making up songs and singing along. She also loved to listen to her father's collection of classic rock albums, and to imitate the singers she admired. She was especially drawn to the Beatles, who inspired her to write her own lyrics and to experiment with different genres.

Taylor's musical journey continued when she was in elementary school, and she joined the choir and the musical theater club. She loved to perform on stage, and to express herself through songs and characters. She also learned to play the guitar, the banjo, and the ukulele, and to explore different styles of music, from country to pop to folk. She wrote songs about her feelings, her experiences, and her dreams, and recorded them on a cassette tape recorder.

Taylor's musical journey reached a turning point when she was 11, and she visited Nashville for the first time. She was amazed by the city's rich musical heritage, and by the opportunities it offered to aspiring artists. She decided to pursue a career in music, and to move to Nashville with her family. She worked hard to improve her skills, to network with industry professionals, and to showcase her talent. She faced many challenges and rejections, but she never gave up on her passion. She eventually landed a record deal, and released her first album, Taylor Swift, when she was 16.

Taylor Swift's musical journey is a remarkable story of passion and perseverance, of creativity and courage, of talent and tenacity. It is a story that shows how music can transform a person's life, and how a person can transform music. It is a story that inspires millions of people around the world, who relate to Taylor's songs and admire her spirit. It is a story that proves that anything is possible, if you follow your heart and chase your dreams.

- *Navigating through trials and triumphs.*

Taylor Swift's story isn't a fairytale ascent to pop stardom. It's a vibrant tapestry, meticulously woven with threads of trials and triumphs. From the tender age of 14, armed with a guitar and a notebook full of dreams, she embarked on a path littered with obstacles.

Early Setbacks: Seeds of Resilience

Rejection stung early. Dropped from a tour at 17, the sting could have turned into bitterness. But Taylor, fueled by an unwavering belief in her music, turned it into resilience. She channeled the hurt into anthems like "Teardrops on My Guitar," resonating with millions who felt unseen and unheard.

Moments of Doubt: The Crossroads of Growth

Even amidst roaring success, self-doubt crept in. The public dissection of her relationships, the ownership of her masters, the pressure to maintain an image – these were battles fought not just in the spotlight, but also in the quiet corners of her soul. Tracks like "All Too Well" and "Miss Americana & The Heartbreak Prince" laid bare these vulnerabilities, showcasing not just pain, but a vulnerability that resonated deeply.

Overcoming Obstacles with Grace and Perseverance

Taylor's response to adversity was never to shrink back. Each challenge became a stepping stone. When ownership of her music was denied, she re-recorded her albums, reclaiming her narrative and empowering other artists to fight for theirs. Through it all, she held her head high, her grace and dignity shining brighter than any negativity.

Breakthroughs and Victories: Shaping the Artist and the Individual

From winning her first Grammy at 18 to her record-breaking album sales, Taylor's career milestones are undeniable. But the true triumphs lie in the evolution they represent. Each award, each sold-out stadium, was a testament to her growth as an artist, pushing boundaries and defying expectations.

Intimate Insights: The Heart of a Songstress

Taylor's music isn't just catchy tunes; it's an open diary. In songs like "Long Live" and "The Story of Us," she shared the elation of victory and the pang of loss with her fans. This rawness fostered a connection that transcended music, making her not just a star, but a confidante, a sister, a friend.

From Trials to Triumph: The Making of an Inspiration

Today, Taylor Swift stands tall, not just as a musical powerhouse, but as an inspiration. Her journey, etched with trials and triumphs, resonates with anyone who's ever dared to dream and faced setbacks. She reminds us that growth comes from embracing vulnerability, that resilience is forged in the fires of adversity, and that ultimately, our stories, flaws and all, are what make us who we are.

Chapter 2: The Road to Nashville

- Ambitions in the country music realm.

Long before pop anthems filled stadiums, a young Taylor Swift dreamt in twang. Country music wasn't just a genre; it was the air she breathed, the soundtrack to her small-town Pennsylvania life. The roots of her passion ran deep, nourished by:

Family Harmony: Surrounded by a family who sang together, music was woven into the fabric of Taylor's existence. Grandparents played country classics, while her mom, herself a songwriter, nurtured Taylor's own musical aspirations.

Storytelling Strings: Dolly Parton's emotional narratives and Shania Twain's feisty anthems resonated with Taylor's budding songwriting sensibilities. Country music's ability to weave tales of love, loss, and resilience struck a chord in her young heart.

Stage Lights Beckoning: At eleven, a performance of LeAnn Rimes' "The Big Phat Party" at a local fair ignited a fire in Taylor. The stage became her dream, the roar of the crowd a melody she craved.

Armed with a guitar and unwavering determination, Taylor embarked on her journey:

Local Heroine: From school talent shows to county fairs, she honed her craft, mesmerizing audiences with her heartfelt lyrics and genuine stage presence. Every performance fueled her ambition, every applause a stepping stone.

Nashville Calling: At 12, armed with a demo and a dream, she descended upon Nashville, the Mecca of country music. Rejections stung, but Taylor's resilience wouldn't be deterred. Open mic nights and songwriting workshops became her classrooms, each challenge a lesson learned.

Pivotal Moments: Signing with RCA at 14 was a validation, but the real turning point came with meeting songwriter Liz Rose. Together, they crafted "Tim McGraw," a poignant ode to lost love that captured the essence of young Taylor and resonated with millions.

The challenges were numerous: navigating a male-dominated industry, balancing school and career, and the ever-present pressure to conform. But Taylor, ever the strategist, countered with:

Authenticity as Armor: She refused to compromise her genuine voice, blending traditional country with her own pop sensibilities. This authenticity resonated with fans, making her relatable and unique.

Songwriting as Sword: Taylor poured her experiences, both joyful and heartbreaking, into her music. Each song became a weapon against self-doubt, a shield against criticism, and a bridge to connect with her audience.

Grassroots Grit: While Nashville presented opportunities, Taylor never forgot her roots. Local radio play, fan meet-and-greets, and energetic live shows cemented her connection with her core audience, building a loyal fanbase brick by brick.

Taylor's early years in country music were not a fairytale ascent. They were a testament to raw talent, unwavering determination, and a strategic blend of tradition and innovation. This foundation, built on the fertile ground of Nashville dreams and small-town grit, fueled her rise to become not just a country star, but a global icon. The essence of Taylor's early journey is encapsulated in the lyrics of "Teardrops on My Guitar": "Someday I'll be living in a big ol' city, and all you're ever gonna be is mean." It's a declaration of ambition, a promise whispered to the doubters, a seed sown in the heart of country music that blossomed into a pop music phenomenon.

- Crafting her musical abilities

Taylor Swift's dream was to become a country star, and she pursued it with determination and persistence. She moved to Nashville with her family when she was fourteen, after convincing them to support her musical aspirations. She signed with Sony/ATV Music Publishing as the youngest songwriter ever, and later with Big Machine Records as the youngest artist ever. She released her self-titled debut album in 2006, which featured her first hit single, "Tim McGraw". The album was a commercial and critical success, earning her a Grammy nomination for Best New Artist, and establishing her as a rising star in the country music scene.

Taylor Swift's musical journey did not stop there. She continued to hone her musical abilities, and to explore new genres and sounds. She released her second album, Fearless, in 2008, which was a crossover success, blending country and pop elements. The album won four Grammy Awards, including Album of the Year, making her the youngest artist to win the award. She also embarked on her first headlining tour, which sold out venues around the world. She followed up with her third album, Spcak Now, in 2010, which was entirely written by her, and showcased her growth as a songwriter and storyteller. The album was another smash hit, selling over one million copies in its first week, and spawning hits like "Mine", "Back to December", and "Mean".

Taylor Swift's musical journey was not without challenges and obstacles. She faced criticism, backlash, and controversy from various sources, such as the media, the public, and other artists. She also had to deal with the pressures and expectations of fame, as well as the scrutiny and invasion of her personal life. She overcame these difficulties by staying true to herself, working hard, and expressing herself through her music. She also used her platform to advocate for causes she cared about, such as education, feminism, and LGBTQ+ rights.

Taylor Swift's musical journey was also marked by innovation and experimentation. She released her fourth album, Red, in 2012, which incorporated elements of rock, folk, and electronic music. The album was praised for its diversity and maturity, and featured hits like "We Are Never Ever Getting Back Together", "I Knew You Were Trouble", and "22". She then released her fifth album, 1989, in 2014, which was her first full-fledged pop album, and a departure from her country roots. The album was a massive success, selling over 10 million copies worldwide, and winning three Grammy Awards, including Album of the Year. It also spawned hits like "Shake It Off", "Blank Space", and "Bad Blood".

Taylor Swift's musical journey reached new heights with her sixth album, Reputation, in 2017, which was her darkest and most personal album to date. The album addressed themes such as reputation, media, and love, and featured a more edgy and experimental sound, influenced by hip hop, R&B, and electro-pop. The album was a critical and commercial triumph, selling over two million copies in its first week, and breaking several records. It also featured hits like "Look What You Made Me Do", "...Ready For It?", and "Delicate".

Taylor Swift's musical journey took a surprising turn with her seventh album, Lover, in 2019, which was her most romantic and optimistic album to date. The album was a return to her pop roots, with a more colorful and upbeat sound, influenced by synth-pop, indie-pop, and country-pop. The album was a fan and critic favorite, selling over three million copies worldwide, and earning a Grammy nomination for Best Pop Vocal Album. It also featured hits like "ME!", "You Need To Calm Down", and "Lover".

Taylor Swift's musical journey reached a new level of creativity and productivity with her eighth and ninth albums, Folklore and Evermore, in 2020, which were surprise releases during the COVID-19 pandemic. The albums were a departure from her previous pop sound, and a return to her folk and country roots, with a more intimate and acoustic sound, influenced by indie-folk, alternative-rock, and chamber-pop. The albums were hailed as her best and most mature works, earning universal acclaim and commercial success. They also won her several awards, including a Grammy for Album of the Year for Folklore, making her the first female artist to win the award three times. They also featured hits like "Cardigan", "Exile", and "Willow".

Taylor Swift's musical journey is an inspiring and impressive story of passion, dedication, and excellence. She has developed her musical abilities from a young age, and has never stopped learning, growing, and evolving as an artist. She has explored various genres and sounds, and has created her own musical identity and legacy. She has faced and overcome many challenges and obstacles, and has used her music as a way of expressing herself and connecting with others. She has achieved remarkable success and recognition, and has influenced and inspired millions of fans and musicians around the world. She is a musical icon, and a living legend.

- The serendipitous moment of discovery.

Taylor Swift had always loved music, but she never imagined that one day she would become one of the biggest stars in the world. She was just a 14-year-old girl from Pennsylvania, who had moved to Nashville with her family to pursue her dream of becoming a country singer. She had signed a development deal with RCA Records, but she was not satisfied with the songs they wanted her to record. She wanted to write her own songs, and express her own voice.

One day, she was performing at a songwriter's showcase at the Bluebird Cafe, a famous venue for aspiring musicians. She was nervous, but she sang her heart out, hoping to impress someone in the audience. Little did she know that someone was Scott Borchetta, a former executive at DreamWorks Records, who was looking for new talent for his own label, Big Machine Records. He was captivated by Taylor's voice, her lyrics, and her charisma. He approached her after the show, and offered her a recording contract on the spot.

Taylor was stunned, but also thrilled. She felt like this was the opportunity she had been waiting for, the chance to make her own music, and to reach a wider audience. She accepted the offer, and became the first artist to sign with Big Machine Records. She was excited, but also nervous.

She wondered if she was ready for this big step, and if she could live up to the expectations. She also knew that she had to work hard, and prove herself in the competitive industry.

Taylor's serendipitous moment at the Bluebird Cafe was the beginning of her meteoric rise to fame. She released her self-titled debut album in 2006, which featured her first hit single, "Tim McGraw". The album was a commercial and critical success, earning her a Grammy nomination for Best New Artist, and establishing her as a rising star in the country music scene. She followed up with her second album, Fearless, in 2008, which was a crossover success, blending country and pop elements. The album won four Grammy Awards, including Album of the Year, making her the youngest artist to win the award. She also embarked on her first headlining tour, which sold out venues around the world.

Taylor's talent discovery at the Bluebird Cafe was a transformative moment in her life, and in her career. It ignited her passion for music, and opened doors to new opportunities. It also introduced her to Scott Borchetta, who became her mentor, her friend, and her partner in her musical journey. It was a moment of magic and serendipity, that shaped Taylor's journey to stardom.

Chapter 3: Fearless and Fabulous

- Swift's meteoric rise to international acclaim.

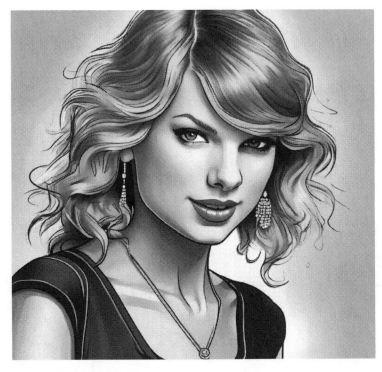

Few journeys in music are as captivating as Taylor Swift's. From strumming guitar in cafes to captivating stadiums worldwide, her rise to international superstardom is a testament to talent, hard work, and a unique connection with fans. Let's embark on a journey tracing the key milestones and decisions that propelled her to the top:

Country Darling Takes Flight:

Small-town beginnings: Taylor's story starts in rural Pennsylvania, fueled by a passion for songwriting and a relentless pursuit of her dreams. Early performances at fairs and talent shows laid the foundation for her musical journey.

Nashville hustle: Relocating to Nashville at 14, Taylor immersed herself in the country music scene, honing her craft and writing songs that resonated with authenticity and relatable emotions.

Chart-topping hits: Her self-titled debut album launched her into the spotlight, anthems like "Tim McGraw" and "Teardrops on My Guitar" resonating with millions. Subsequent albums like "Fearless" and "Speak Now" cemented her status as a country music powerhouse.

Crossing Genres, Breaking Barriers:

Experimentation and evolution: While remaining true to her storytelling roots, Taylor's artistry blossomed, incorporating pop elements into albums like "Red" and "1989," defying genre limitations and expanding her audience.

Strategic collaborations: Partnering with renowned artists like Ed Sheeran and Kendrick Lamar broadened her musical horizons and introduced her to new listeners, showcasing her versatility and willingness to explore.

Embracing technology: Taylor capitalized on emerging platforms like YouTube and social media, forging a direct connection with fans and fostering a dedicated community.

Navigating the Spotlight:

From wide-eyed wonder to self-assured artist: Taylor's initial excitement at fame gradually matured into a more guarded approach, navigating the challenges of scrutiny and public perception with grace and dignity.

Using her voice for good: Leveraging her platform, Taylor spoke out on issues like artist ownership and equality, inspiring fans and advocating for positive change.

Staying true to her roots: Despite global success, Taylor maintained a connection to her country music roots, performing at iconic events like the Grand Ole Opry and collaborating with country legends.

Impact and Legacy:

A relatable icon: Taylor's music connects with audiences across generations and cultures, her lyrics capturing the complexities of love, loss, and self-discovery.

Storytelling prowess: Her ability to weave personal narratives into universal themes resonates deeply, fostering a sense of community and shared experience among fans.

A force for change: Taylor's influence extends beyond music, inspiring young people to embrace their individuality, chase their dreams, and advocate for what they believe in.

Taylor Swift's journey is an ongoing testament to the power of talent, dedication, and genuine connection. From chart-topping hits to genre-bending experimentation, her music continues to evolve, captivating audiences worldwide. Her story serves as an inspiration to aspiring artists and dreamers everywhere, proving that with passion, perseverance, and a touch of Taylor's signature storytelling magic, even the most audacious dreams can take flight.

- The emotive core of her lyrical expressions.

Taylor Swift's music isn't just catchy tunes; it's an emotional journey woven into lyrics that resonate with millions. Let's explore the heart of her artistry, where stories unfold and feelings find voice:

Themes Deeply Personal:

Love in All Its Forms: From the innocent butterflies of "Fifteen" to the bittersweet nostalgia of "All Too Well," Taylor paints love in its myriad hues, capturing the joy, heartache, and everything in between.

Resilience in the Face of Heartbreak: Songs like "Shake It Off" and "Delicate" showcase her ability to find strength and self-worth amidst pain, empowering listeners to rise above their own challenges.

Finding Your Voice and Identity: Anthems like "Speak Now" and "Fearless" celebrate self-discovery and embracing individuality, inspiring young listeners to be themselves unapologetically.

Creative Process: From Raw Emotion to Masterpiece:

Finding Inspiration Everywhere: From personal experiences to daydreams, Taylor draws inspiration from life itself, transforming these moments into relatable narratives.

Wordplay with Powerful Intent: She wields language with precision, choosing words that not only evoke emotions but also paint vivid pictures and tell intricate stories.

Crafting Stories that Connect: Each song unfolds like a miniature novel, immersing listeners in relatable characters, emotions, and experiences.

Storytelling Techniques that Captivate:

Masterful Use of Imagery: Her lyrics paint pictures with words, transporting listeners to specific locations, feelings, and memories with incredible detail.

Honest Vulnerability: Taylor bares her soul in her songs, sharing emotions both joyful and painful, creating a deep sense of connection with her audience.

Universality in the Specific: By weaving personal experiences into broader themes, Taylor's music resonates with listeners across cultures and generations.

Impact on Fans: More Than Just Lyrics:

A Soundtrack for Life: Fans find solace, strength, and celebration in her music, using it as a companion for their own journeys.

Building a Community: Taylor's lyrics foster a sense of shared experience, creating a global community of fans who connect through her music.

Finding Empowerment Through Shared Emotion: By expressing complex emotions honestly, Taylor empowers fans to navigate their own feelings and find their voices.

Taylor Swift's lyrics are more than just words on a page; they're emotional tapestries woven from personal experiences and crafted with meticulous detail. They resonate with millions because they capture the universal language of the heart, offering solace, strength, and a sense of belonging. Her music is a testament to the power of storytelling and the profound impact artists can have on their audiences, reminding us that even the most personal emotions can connect us all.

- Coping mechanisms amidst the glare of fame.

Taylor Swift has demonstrated remarkable resilience in navigating the intense scrutiny and pressures of fame. Despite the relentless spotlight, she has developed various coping mechanisms to maintain her mental and emotional well-being.

One key strategy Taylor employs is mindfulness practices. She has spoken openly about the importance of staying present and grounded amidst the chaos of fame. Taylor incorporates meditation, journaling, and other mindfulness techniques into her daily routine to center herself and manage stress.

Additionally, Taylor leans on her support system of loved ones. She has cultivated strong relationships with family and friends who provide her with unconditional love and support. Taylor often seeks advice and comfort from those closest to her, finding solace in their understanding and empathy.

Balancing her public persona with her personal life is undoubtedly a challenge for Taylor. She faces constant scrutiny and judgment from the media and the public, which can take a toll on her mental health. However, she remains authentic and true to herself, refusing to compromise her values or integrity for the sake of fame.

Taylor also prioritizes self-care and boundaries to protect her well-being. She recognizes the importance of taking breaks, setting limits on her time and energy, and prioritizing activities that bring her joy and fulfillment outside of her career.

Despite the pressures of fame, Taylor has shown incredible strength and grace in overcoming adversity. She has weathered numerous controversies and setbacks with resilience, using these experiences as opportunities for growth and self-reflection.

Chapter 4: Speak Now and Red

- Exploring the evolution of her musical palette.

Taylor Swift's musical journey is a fascinating exploration of artistic evolution and creative reinvention. It all began with her roots in country music, where she drew inspiration from classic artists like Dolly Parton and Shania Twain.

Taylor's early albums, such as "Taylor Swift" and "Fearless," showcased her knack for storytelling and heartfelt lyricism, grounded in the traditions of country music.

As her career progressed, Taylor began to experiment with new sounds and genres, paving the way for her transition into pop music. Albums like "Red" and "1989" marked significant milestones in Taylor's musical evolution, blending elements of pop, rock, and electronic music to create a fresh and dynamic sound. The production became more layered and polished, reflecting Taylor's growing confidence and ambition as an artist.

The creative process behind each album is deeply personal for Taylor. She often draws inspiration from her own experiences and emotions, crafting songs that resonate with authenticity and vulnerability. From the conceptualization of themes to the production of innovative sounds and arrangements, Taylor is intimately involved in every aspect of her music-making process.

Pivotal albums and collaborations have played a significant role in shaping Taylor's musical evolution. Collaborations with artists like Jack Antonoff and Max Martin have pushed boundaries and introduced new sonic landscapes to Taylor's music. Each album represents a new chapter in Taylor's artistic journey, showcasing her versatility and depth as a musician and songwriter.

Taylor's growth as a musician and songwriter is evident in her willingness to take risks and defy expectations. With each new project, she continues to push the boundaries of her sound, exploring new genres and styles while remaining true to her core identity as an artist. From country roots to pop dominance, Taylor Swift's musical palette is a vibrant tapestry of creativity and innovation, illustrating the richness and diversity of her evolving sound.

- Maturation in songwriting.

Taylor Swift's songwriting journey is a captivating tapestry woven with threads of growth, experimentation, and unwavering vulnerability. Let's delve into the evolution of her lyrical prowess, uncovering the themes, influences, and life experiences that have shaped her voice as a storyteller:

Early Days: Innocence & Storytelling Charm:

Country Beginnings: Her early albums like "Fearless" and "Speak Now" brim with youthful energy, capturing the innocent joys and heartbreaks of teenage life.

Storytelling Through Vivid Detail: Songs like "Fifteen" and "Teardrops on My Guitar" paint relatable narratives with precise imagery, making listeners feel like they're living every moment.

Themes of Love & Loss: Love, in all its forms, takes center stage. From puppy love anthems to bittersweet breakups, Taylor captures the emotional rollercoaster of young relationships.

Shifting Gears: Introspection & Expanding Horizons:

Genre-Bending Experimentation: Albums like "Red" and "1989" showcase a move towards pop influences, reflecting a more nuanced and mature perspective.

Deeper Dive into Emotions: The lyrical focus shifts from external events to internal struggles, exploring themes of self-doubt, personal growth, and navigating adulthood.

Social Commentary Emerges: Songs like "Blank Space" and "Shake It Off" address societal pressures and media portrayals, showcasing Taylor's growing awareness of the world around her.

Vulnerability & Authenticity: Laying Bare Her Soul:

Confessional & Personal Lyrics: Albums like "Reputation" and "Lover" mark a shift towards even more personal revelations, delving into vulnerability with unflinching honesty.

Mental Health Advocacy: Songs like "Delicate" and "Miss Americana & The Heartbreak Prince" openly discuss struggles with anxiety and societal expectations, sparking important conversations.

Experimentation with Form & Genre: "Folklore" and "Evermore" showcase artistic daring, exploring storytelling through mythical narratives and shifting between musical styles seamlessly.

Pushing Boundaries & Breaking Conventions:

Mastering Storytelling Techniques: Taylor's use of metaphors, symbolism, and vivid imagery continues to refine, creating even deeper emotional connections with listeners.

Genre-Defying Exploration: Recent releases like "Carolina" and "Anti-Hero" demonstrate her willingness to defy genre expectations, proving her artistry knows no bounds.

Addressing Societal Issues: From gender equality in "The Man" to political commentary in "Only The Young," Taylor continues to use her platform to advocate for change.

The Ever-Evolving Storyteller:

Taylor Swift's songwriting journey is far from over. Each album unveils a new facet of her emotional growth, tackling complex themes with vulnerability and authenticity. Her music resonates deeply because it reflects the universal experiences of love, loss, and self-discovery. As she continues to experiment and push boundaries, one thing remains constant: Taylor's ability to lay bare her soul, captivating audiences with the raw power of her words and melodies. Her evolving artistry serves as a testament to the transformative power of songwriting, reminding us that growth and change are the cornerstones of true artistic expression.

- *Media scrutiny and its impact.*

Taylor Swift's rise to fame has been as meteoric as the media spotlight that has followed her every step. But the glitter of fame rarely hides the sting of scrutiny, and Taylor's journey is a poignant example of the complexities and challenges that come with being under constant observation.

Facing the Glare:

 Tabloid Tales and Paparazzi Intrusions: From dissected relationships to fabricated rumors, Taylor has been a constant target of tabloid sensationalism and invasive paparazzi tactics.

Shifting Narratives and Public Perception: Media narratives have often shaped public perception, painting her as everything from "America's Sweetheart" to a vengeful villain, rarely capturing the full picture.

The Toll on Mental Wellbeing: The relentless scrutiny has taken a toll on Taylor's mental and emotional well-being, as she has openly discussed struggling with anxiety and self-doubt.

Strategies for Navigating the Storm:

Taking Control of the Narrative: Through her music and social media presence, Taylor has increasingly sought to control her own narrative, sharing her truth and perspectives directly with fans.

Speaking Out Against Misogyny and Double Standards: She has used her platform to advocate against the unfair treatment and double standards often faced by women in the public eye.

Finding Sanctuary in Music and Community: Her songwriting becomes a cathartic outlet, processing experiences and emotions while her dedicated fanbase offers unwavering support.

Resilience and the Lessons Learned:

Rising Above the Noise: Despite the challenges, Taylor's resilience shines through. She has learned to navigate the complexities of fame, using her experiences to inspire others facing similar scrutiny.

The Importance of Self-Care and Setting Boundaries: Recognizing the impact on her well-being, Taylor prioritizes self-care and sets boundaries to protect her privacy and mental health.

Reclaiming Her Power: Through her artistic evolution and open communication, Taylor continues to reclaim her power, demonstrating the importance of self-ownership and finding strength in vulnerability.

Taylor Swift's story is a reminder that the human cost of fame can be high. Yet, it's also a testament to the power of resilience and finding one's voice amidst the noise. As she continues to navigate the complexities of media scrutiny, her journey serves as a valuable lesson in self-compassion, setting boundaries, and reclaiming power in the face of adversity. It's a story that resonates not just with celebrities, but with anyone who has ever felt judged or misrepresented, offering hope and inspiration for finding strength and authenticity in the face of scrutiny.

Chapter 5: 1989 and Reputation

- Transition into pop music dominance.

Taylor Swift's transition from country music sensation to pop music dominance marked a monumental shift in her career and solidified her status as a pop icon. This transformation was driven by a combination of artistic evolution, creative experimentation, and a desire to challenge herself and push boundaries.

The catalysts behind Taylor's decision to shift her musical direction were multifaceted. As she matured as an artist, Taylor felt a natural inclination to explore new sounds and genres, seeking to expand her creative horizons beyond the confines of country music. Additionally, she was inspired by the pop music landscape and saw an opportunity to reach a broader audience with her music.

Strategic moves and collaborations played a crucial role in propelling Taylor's transition to pop music dominance. Albums like "Red" and "1989" showcased her ability to seamlessly blend elements of pop, rock, and electronic music, resulting in chart-topping singles and critical acclaim. Collaborations with renowned producers and songwriters, such as Max Martin and Jack Antonoff, helped Taylor refine her sound and elevate her music to new heights.

However, Taylor's transition to pop music was not without its challenges. She faced skepticism and scrutiny from industry insiders and fans alike, who questioned her ability to successfully navigate a new genre. Additionally, there was pressure to redefine her public image and shed the country music label that had defined her early career.

Despite these challenges, Taylor's transition to pop music proved to be a triumph. Her groundbreaking albums and chart-topping singles solidified her position as a global superstar and expanded her influence far beyond the country music scene. Taylor's pop music breakthroughs not only redefined her career trajectory but also set a new standard for innovation and creativity within the genre.

Today, Taylor Swift continues to push boundaries and innovate within the pop music landscape. With each new project, she explores new sonic territories and pushes the limits of her artistic expression, cementing her legacy as one of the most influential pop icons of her generation.

- Dealing with public controversies.

Taylor Swift's journey through public controversies has been a testament to her resilience, grace, and determination to stay true to herself amidst intense scrutiny. Throughout her career, she has faced a myriad of controversies and scandals, ranging from public feuds to tabloid rumors, yet she has consistently navigated these challenges with poise and integrity.

One of the most notable controversies Taylor faced was the infamous feud with Kanye West and Kim Kardashian. The feud erupted over Kanye's song "Famous," which included derogatory lyrics about Taylor that she claimed she had not approved. This controversy played out publicly, with Taylor being painted as a villain in the media. However, she addressed the situation head-on, speaking out about the importance of artistic integrity and standing up for oneself in the face of injustice.

Another significant controversy arose during the MeToo movement when Taylor bravely came forward with her own experiences of sexual harassment and assault. Her decision to speak out sparked important conversations about consent and empowerment in the music industry and beyond. Taylor's advocacy for survivors of sexual violence showcased her willingness to use her platform for social good and shed light on important issues.

Throughout these controversies, Taylor has employed various strategies for handling public scrutiny with grace and resilience. She has often taken to social media to address rumors and set the record straight, using her platform to communicate directly with her fans and the public. Additionally, Taylor has been open and candid in interviews, sharing her perspective and experiences in a thoughtful and articulate manner.

However, navigating public controversies has undoubtedly taken an emotional toll on Taylor. The constant scrutiny and judgment from the media and the public can be overwhelming, yet she has remained steadfast in her commitment to staying true to herself and her values. Through these experiences, Taylor has learned valuable lessons about resilience and perseverance, emerging stronger and more resilient with each challenge she faces.

Ultimately, Taylor Swift's journey through public controversies is a nuanced portrait of the complexities of fame and the power of staying true to oneself amidst public scrutiny. Her ability to navigate these challenges with grace and integrity has only strengthened her bond with her fans and solidified her status as a role model for resilience and authenticity.

- Pinnacle moments and groundbreaking achievements.

Taylor Swift's career is a constellation of shining moments, each one marking a significant triumph in her meteoric rise to the top. Let's explore some of these defining stars, illuminating the stories, emotions, and impact behind them:

Early Sparkles:

Grammy Breakthrough: At 20, Taylor became the youngest person ever to win the Album of the Year Grammy for "Fearless," solidifying her arrival as a force to be reckoned with. The win, filled with both shock and joy, symbolized the power of storytelling and resonated with millions.

Record-Breaking Sales: "Red" became the first album in Billboard history to sell over a million copies in its first week, a testament to her loyal fanbase and the universal appeal of her music. The achievement, fuelled by tireless promotion and genuine connection with fans, redefined expectations for female artists.

Genre-Bending Leap:

From Country Darling to Pop Icon: The release of "1989" marked a bold artistic shift, embracing pop elements and captivating a global audience. The album, fueled by creative collaborations and strategic marketing, challenged genre boundaries and propelled Taylor to international superstardom.

The "Shake It Off" Phenomenon: This empowering anthem shattered records and became a cultural touchstone, resonating with anyone who had faced criticism or negativity. The song, born from personal struggles, transformed into a global symbol of resilience and self-belief.

Awards and Legacy:

Becoming the Decade's Most Awarded Artist: With numerous Grammy wins, including Song of the Year three times, Taylor cemented her place as a songwriting powerhouse. Beyond the accolades, these awards recognized the emotional depth and artistry woven into her music.

The Stadium Tour Experience: From sold-out shows to elaborate stage productions, Taylor's tours redefined the concert experience, showcasing her incredible artistry and dedication to connecting with fans on a grand scale. These tours transcended entertainment, becoming immersive journeys through her music and stories.

Impact and Inspiration:

Using Her Platform: Taylor has consistently used her voice to advocate for social issues, from LGBTQ+ rights to artist ownership. This commitment to speaking out empowers her fans and sparks important conversations, proving that influence can extend beyond music.

Inspiring a Generation of Songwriters: Her lyrical honesty and storytelling prowess have influenced countless aspiring artists, encouraging them to embrace vulnerability and express themselves authentically. She inspires them to not only dream big, but to actively pursue those dreams.

These are just a few of the countless shining moments that illuminate Taylor Swift's extraordinary career. Each one highlights her unwavering dedication, relentless creativity, and genuine connection with her audience. More than just awards and sales, these moments showcase her impact on the music industry and popular culture, inspiring millions to find their voice and chase their dreams, proving that even the brightest stars started as tiny sparks of talent and passion.

Chapter 6: Lover and Miss Americana

- Embracing joy and contentment.

Taylor Swift's journey of embracing joy and contentment amidst the highs and lows of fame is a testament to her resilience, mindfulness, and commitment to self-care.

Throughout her career, Taylor has experienced moments of happiness and fulfillment both personally and professionally, finding love, pursuing passion projects, and embracing gratitude amidst the demands of her career.

One of the key strategies Taylor employs to cultivate a sense of joy and contentment is mindfulness. She has spoken openly about the importance of staying present and grounded amidst the chaos of fame, incorporating practices like meditation and journaling into her daily routine. By prioritizing mindfulness, Taylor is able to maintain a sense of perspective and gratitude, even in the face of challenges.

Taylor also prioritizes self-care, recognizing the importance of taking breaks and setting boundaries to protect her well-being. Whether it's spending time with loved ones, indulging in hobbies, or simply resting and recharging, Taylor makes time for activities that bring her joy and fulfillment outside of her career.

Despite the pressures of fame, Taylor has learned valuable lessons about the importance of balance and perspective. She has navigated challenges with resilience and grace, using setbacks as opportunities for growth and self-reflection. Taylor understands that true happiness comes from within, and she is committed to living authentically and staying true to herself amidst the whirlwind of fame.

Embracing joy and contentment has had a profound impact on Taylor's creativity and well-being. By prioritizing happiness and fulfillment, she is able to tap into her creativity more freely and produce work that resonates with authenticity and emotion. Taylor shares these values with her fans, using her platform to promote positivity, self-love, and gratitude.

- Taylor's advocacy for various causes.

Taylor Swift's passionate advocacy for a diverse range of causes is deeply rooted in her personal experiences, values, and sense of responsibility as a public figure. Throughout her career, Taylor has used her platform to amplify marginalized voices, raise awareness about important issues, and inspire positive change in the world.

Motivated by her own experiences with inequality and injustice, Taylor has been a vocal advocate for gender equality, LGBTQ+ rights, and other social justice causes. She understands the power of her platform and the responsibility that comes with it, recognizing that she has the ability to spark meaningful conversations and drive real change.

One of the causes Taylor has championed is gender equality, using her voice and influence to advocate for equal rights and opportunities for women and girls. She has supported organizations like the Women's March and Time's Up, using her platform to raise awareness about gender-based discrimination and promote empowerment and inclusivity.

Taylor has also been a staunch ally for the LGBTQ+ community, speaking out in support of marriage equality and LGBTQ+ rights. She has used her music, public appearances, and social media platforms to advocate for acceptance, love, and equality for all individuals, regardless of sexual orientation or gender identity.

In addition to her vocal advocacy, Taylor has taken tangible actions to support causes close to her heart. She has made generous donations to organizations working to promote social justice and equality, and has used her influence to encourage others to get involved and make a difference.

Taylor's advocacy work has had a significant impact on her fans and followers, inspiring them to become more engaged in social issues and take action in their own communities. Through her authenticity, passion, and dedication, Taylor has shown that anyone can make a difference, no matter how big or small their platform may be.

- Sharing her personal odyssey with the world.

Moments of Vulnerability:

Lyrics as Diaries: Swift's lyrics act as raw, emotional diaries. Tracks like "All Too Well" and "Dear John" lay bare the sting of heartbreak, while "Long Live" and "Story of Us" capture the bittersweetness of young love. This vulnerability creates a unique intimacy with fans, who find solace in shared experiences.

Beyond Music: Interviews and social media offer glimpses into her life beyond songs. The vulnerability expressed in her Netflix documentary "Miss Americana" resonated deeply, showcasing her struggles with public scrutiny and ownership of her music.

Themes and Narratives:

Love's Many Faces: Love, in all its complexities, forms a cornerstone of Swift's music. From the starry-eyed infatuation of "Teardrops on My Guitar" to the mature reflection of "Lover," she explores love's joys and heartbreaks, creating relatable anthems for every stage of life.

Self-Discovery and Growth: As she evolves, so do her narratives. From the confident independence of "Shake It Off" to the self-assured "ME!," Swift documents her journey of self-discovery, inspiring fans to embrace their own individuality.

Resilience in the Face of Challenges: Swift hasn't shied away from sharing adversity. Songs like "Mean" and

"Innocent" address public scrutiny and criticism head-on, demonstrating her resilience and inspiring fans to overcome their own challenges.

Challenges and Rewards of Sharing:

Navigating Public Scrutiny: Sharing personal experiences comes with inevitable public scrutiny. Swift has faced criticism and media judgment, navigating the complexities of fame and protecting her privacy.

Connecting with Fans: Despite the challenges, the rewards are profound. Her openness fosters a deep connection with fans, who see themselves reflected in her stories and find solace and strength in shared experiences.

Impact and Inspiration:

Authenticity Breeds Connection: Swift's honesty resonates with audiences globally, transcending cultural barriers. Her willingness to be vulnerable fosters a sense of community and shared understanding, reminding fans they're not alone.

Empowering Through Storytelling: By sharing her journey, Swift empowers others to embrace their own narratives. Tracks like "The Man" and "Miss Americana & The Heartbreak Prince" advocate for female empowerment and inspire fans to use their voices.

A Nuanced Portrait:

Taylor Swift's journey isn't black and white. It's a tapestry woven with vulnerability, growth, and the challenges of sharing one's life with the world. Yet, her courage and authenticity have not only shaped her career but also empowered millions to embrace their own stories, proving that sharing our personal odysseys can be a source of connection, inspiration, and strength.

Chapter 7: Folklore and Evermore

- Surprising departures in musical style.

Taylor Swift's musical journey isn't a stroll down a predictable path; it's a daring leap into unexplored sonic territories, each landing solidifying her place as a genre-bending powerhouse. Let's delve into the fascinating moments where she defied expectations, leaving behind the familiar for the electrifying unknown.

From Country Crooner to Pop Queen:

Sparks Ignite: The embers of change glowed in "Speak Now," with hints of synth-pop peeking through the acoustic guitars. But "Red" was the explosion, a vibrant tapestry of pop anthems ("We Are Never Ever Getting Back Together") and emotional ballads ("All Too Well"), propelled by collaborations with Max Martin and Shellback. It wasn't just a shift; it was a sonic rebellion, leaving Nashville in the rearview mirror.

Unveiling "1989": A Pop Kaleidoscope:

Breaking the Mold: "1989" shattered genre boundaries. Gone were the twangy guitars, replaced by pulsating synths and infectious hooks ("Shake It Off"). Each track, from the synth-heavy "Blank Space" to the dreamy "Wildest Dreams," was a sonic adventure, drawing inspiration from 80s pop icons like Michael Jackson and Madonna.

Folklore's Whispered Revolution:

Whispers from the Unknown: The pandemic became the unexpected muse for "folklore." Stripped bare of pop's glitz, the album embraced an intimate acoustic soundscape ("cardigan"), drawing heavily from indie rock and alternative influences like The National. It was a surprise departure, yet a resounding success, earning critical acclaim and solidifying her artistic versatility.

Evermore: Deepening the Exploration:

Pushing the Boundaries Further: Building on "folklore's" introspective nature, "evermore" ventured even deeper, incorporating darker folk and chamber pop elements ("willow"). Collaborations with Aaron Dessner continued to shape the sound, showcasing her willingness to experiment and defy categorization.

The Creative Spark: Where Inspiration Ignites:

Personal Journeys Fueling Artistic Evolution: Each musical shift reflects personal growth. "Red" mirrored the fiery emotions of heartbreak, while "1989" embodied her newfound independence. "folklore" emerged from isolation and introspection, while "evermore" delved into themes of loss and resilience. Life experiences become brushstrokes, painting her sonic canvas.

Beyond Inspiration: The Collaborative Tapestry:

A Symphony of Talent: Taylor's journey isn't a solo flight. Collaborators like Max Martin, Jack Antonoff, and Aaron Dessner play crucial roles. They challenge her, push her boundaries, and bring their unique sonic palettes to the table, resulting in a rich and ever-evolving sound.

Impact and Legacy: Redefining What It Means to Be an Artist:

Beyond Genres, Beyond Expectations: Each departure defied expectations, challenging both fans and critics. But this very unpredictability is her strength. She doesn't fit neatly into a box; she creates her own genre, inspiring others to do the same.

Chart-Topping Reinvention: Each shift has been met with commercial success, proving that artistic evolution doesn't have to come at the expense of popularity. She's cemented her place as a force in the industry, influencing countless musicians with her artistic bravery.

A Portrait of a True Trailblazer:

Taylor Swift's musical journey is more than just a collection of hit albums; it's a testament to artistic courage. She doesn't shy away from the unknown, embracing experimentation and challenging herself with each new endeavor. This constant evolution, fueled by personal experiences, artistic curiosity, and collaborative brilliance, has cemented her place as a true musical trailblazer, reminding us that the greatest journeys are often the ones that take us to unexpected destinations.

- Creative resilience amidst the pandemic.

When the world shut down, many artists faltered. But Taylor Swift, as always, found a way to adapt, innovate, and thrive. Let's explore her remarkable display of creative resilience during the pandemic, a testament to her artistic spirit and profound connection with her fans.

From Studios to Screens: Embracing Remote Collaboration:

Zoom Sessions and Digital Diaries: With tours cancelled, Taylor turned to technology. "folklore" and "evermore" were crafted through remote collaborations with producers like Aaron Dessner, exchanging song ideas and recordings virtually. These "quarantine albums" became testaments to the power of creative adaptation.

Virtual Stages and Digital Connections:

 Long Pond Studio Sessions and Folklore: The Long Pond Studio Sessions: As a replacement for live shows, Taylor hosted intimate virtual performances like the "Long Pond Studio Sessions," offering fans a glimpse into the creative process behind "folklore." These events provided a sense of connection and community despite the physical distance.

Pandemic Echoes in Lyrics and Melodies:

  Themes of Isolation and Connection: "folklore" and "evermore" resonated deeply with pandemic experiences. Tracks like "cardigan" and "willow" explored themes of isolation, longing, and the search for connection, mirroring the collective emotions of a world in lockdown.

A Personal Journey of Reflection and Growth:

Finding Solace in Storytelling: While navigating the challenges of the pandemic, Taylor poured her personal experiences into her music. These albums served as a form of self-reflection and emotional processing, offering relatable narratives for fans navigating similar struggles.

Impact and Inspiration: A Beacon of Hope:

Providing Solace and Community: Taylor's music became a source of comfort and connection for fans during a difficult time. The vulnerability and relatability of her lyrics offered solace and a sense of shared experience, fostering a stronger sense of community despite physical limitations.

Inspiring Creative Adaptation: Her innovative approach to creating and connecting with fans during the pandemic became a model for other artists, showcasing the power of adapting and embracing new technologies to stay connected with audiences.

A Portrait of Unwavering Spirit:

Taylor Swift's journey through the pandemic is a testament to the power of creativity, resilience, and connection. She didn't let the limitations define her; instead, she embraced them, emerging stronger and more connected with her fans than ever before. Her story serves as an inspiration to artists and individuals alike, reminding us that even in the face of adversity, creativity can find a way to bloom, connect, and offer solace.

- Collaborative ventures and artistic experimentation.

Taylor Swift's career is marked by dynamic collaborative ventures and bold artistic experimentation that have continually pushed boundaries and expanded horizons in the music industry. From her early days as a country-pop sensation to her evolution into a global pop icon, Swift has consistently sought out innovative partnerships and embraced creative risks.

One of the defining characteristics of Taylor Swift's collaborations is their diversity. She has worked with a wide range of artists, producers, and creatives spanning various genres and generations. From collaborating with established icons like Ed Sheeran and Brendon Urie to championing emerging talents like Phoebe Bridgers and HAIM, Swift has demonstrated a commitment to fostering diversity and inclusion within the industry.

Motivations behind these collaborations vary, reflecting Swift's desire to explore new musical territories and connect with different audiences. Whether it's collaborating with rapper Kendrick Lamar on "Bad Blood" or teaming up with indie folk duo The Civil Wars on "Safe & Sound," Swift's collaborations are driven by a genuine passion for experimentation and a willingness to challenge herself creatively.

The creative process behind Taylor Swift's collaborative ventures is characterized by a collaborative exchange of ideas and experimentation. Swift often draws inspiration from her collaborators, allowing their unique perspectives to influence her own creative vision. From the initial spark of inspiration to the recording studio sessions, Swift fosters an environment of open communication and mutual respect, resulting in dynamic and innovative musical collaborations.

These collaborations have had a profound impact on Taylor Swift's artistic evolution and the broader music landscape. They have allowed her to push boundaries and explore new sonic territories, keeping her sound fresh and relevant with each album release. Moreover, Swift's willingness to collaborate with artists from diverse backgrounds has helped to break down barriers within the industry and promote greater diversity and inclusion.

In summary, Taylor Swift's journey of artistic exploration and collaboration illustrates the power of collaboration and creative risk-taking in shaping her groundbreaking career. Through her diverse range of collaborations and bold artistic experimentation, Swift has continually pushed boundaries, expanded horizons, and cemented her status as one of the most influential artists of her generation.

Chapter 8: Midnights and Eras

- Celebrating the release of her milestone tenth album.

The release of Taylor Swift's milestone tenth album was a momentous occasion celebrated with exhilaration and anticipation by fans worldwide. The journey leading up to the release was filled with excitement, beginning with the initial announcement that Swift was working on new music. As speculation mounted and anticipation grew, Swift teased fans with cryptic clues and hints, building suspense for what would ultimately be a significant moment in her career.

Behind the scenes, meticulous planning and preparation were underway to ensure the album's success. From selecting the tracklist to coordinating promotional efforts, every detail was carefully considered to make the release a standout event. Swift's team worked tirelessly to create buzz and generate excitement, engaging with fans through social media and strategic marketing campaigns.

Thematically, Taylor Swift's milestone album delved into a wide range of concepts and emotions, reflecting her personal journey and artistic evolution. From introspective reflections on love, loss, and resilience to bold statements about empowerment and self-discovery, the album was a testament to Swift's growth as a songwriter and storyteller.

The creative process behind the album was a collaborative effort, with Swift working closely with producers, musicians, and visual artists to bring her vision to life. From the songwriting sessions where Swift poured her heart into crafting honest and relatable lyrics to the production process where she experimented with new sounds and textures, every aspect of the album was infused with creativity and passion.

Visually, the album was accompanied by stunning artwork and imagery that complemented the music's themes and concepts. From the album cover to the music videos and promotional materials, Swift's attention to detail and commitment to storytelling were evident, creating a cohesive and immersive experience for fans.

Upon its release, Taylor Swift's milestone album received an overwhelmingly positive response from both fans and critics alike. Critics praised the album for its bold experimentation, lyrical depth, and infectious melodies, while fans celebrated its relatability and emotional resonance. From heartfelt ballads to infectious pop anthems, the album resonated with audiences worldwide, solidifying Swift's status as one of the most influential artists of her generation.

In conclusion, the celebration surrounding Taylor Swift's milestone tenth album release was a vibrant and joyous occasion, marked by anticipation, excitement, and a sense of achievement. From the initial announcement to the meticulous planning and preparation behind the scenes, every aspect of the release was carefully orchestrated to make it a standout moment in Swift's career. With its themes of personal reflection, bold artistic statements, and universal appeal, the album captured the hearts and minds of fans around the world, cementing Swift's legacy as a true musical icon.

- Pushing boundaries with genre-bending compositions.

Taylor Swift's innovative approach to pushing boundaries with genre-bending compositions has truly set her apart as a trailblazer in the music industry. Throughout her career, Swift has fearlessly defied conventional genres, seamlessly blending diverse musical influences ranging from pop and country to indie and alternative.

One of the defining moments when Taylor Swift challenged stereotypes and embraced genre-bending was with her transition from country to pop music. With albums like "1989" and "reputation," Swift ventured into pop territory while still infusing elements of her country roots into her music. This bold move not only showcased her versatility as an artist but also expanded her audience and solidified her status as a crossover sensation.

Motivations behind Taylor's genre-bending compositions stem from a desire to challenge stereotypes and explore new sonic landscapes. Swift's creative curiosity and fearlessness drive her to experiment with different musical styles and push the boundaries of what is expected from a pop artist. Whether it's incorporating electronic elements into her music or collaborating with artists from diverse backgrounds, Swift is always eager to push the envelope and defy expectations.

The creative process behind Taylor's genre-bending compositions is a collaborative effort that involves drawing inspiration from a variety of sources. From the initial spark of inspiration to the collaborative efforts that bring her vision to life, Swift works closely with producers, musicians, and songwriters to craft innovative and boundary-pushing music. By fostering an environment of open communication and experimentation, Swift ensures that her genre-bending compositions remain authentic and true to her artistic vision.

The impact of Taylor Swift's genre-bending music on her fans and the broader music landscape is undeniable. Her willingness to experiment with different genres and push boundaries has inspired countless artists to do the same, leading to a more diverse and dynamic musical landscape.

Swift's genre-bending compositions have resonated with fans of all ages and backgrounds, showcasing the universal appeal of her music and solidifying her status as one of the most influential artists of her generation.

In conclusion, Taylor Swift's journey of artistic innovation is a testament to the power of creativity, curiosity, and fearlessness in shaping groundbreaking compositions. By defying conventional genres and seamlessly blending diverse musical influences, Swift has set herself apart as a trailblazer in the music industry, inspiring countless artists to push boundaries and defy expectations. With her genre-bending music, Swift continues to captivate audiences worldwide and leave an indelible mark on the musical landscape.

- Ongoing accolades and recognitions.

Taylor Swift's trophy case isn't just overflowing – it's a testament to a career built on artistic evolution, social impact, and an unwavering pursuit of excellence. Let's delve into the ongoing shower of accolades that validate her artistic prowess and explore the significance these recognitions hold within and beyond the music industry.

A Kaleidoscope of Recognition:

Music's Golden Girl: Her 14 Grammy Awards, including a record-breaking four Album of the Year wins, solidify her as one of music's most decorated artists. But the accolades go beyond just the Grammys. From American Music Awards and Billboard Music Awards to MTV Video Music Awards and countless others, Taylor's dominance spans various platforms and genres.

Beyond the Charts: The recognition extends beyond musical achievements. Humanitarian awards like the TIME Person of the Year acknowledge her advocacy for LGBTQ+ rights and artists' ownership of their work. Her inclusion in Forbes' World's Most Powerful Women highlights her cultural and business influence.

Significance of the Accolades:

Validating Impact: Each award is a stamp of approval, validating the impact of her music and message. They affirm her ability to connect with audiences across generations and cultures, solidifying her legacy as a cultural icon.

Fueling Growth: While appreciative, Taylor isn't solely driven by awards. They serve as motivators, pushing her to constantly evolve and innovate, never settling for the status quo. The hunger for artistic growth and excellence remains the true driving force.

Intimate Reactions: Celebration and Reflection:

Moments of Joy: Wins are celebrated with heartfelt speeches and genuine excitement. She shares the spotlight with collaborators, acknowledging the team effort behind her success.

Beyond the Glitter: Beyond the celebratory moments, Taylor reflects on the deeper meaning of awards. They represent the dedication of her fans, the validation of her artistic choices, and the responsibility to use her platform for positive change.

Continuing Commitment to Excellence:

Inspiration for Aspiring Artists: Her journey serves as an inspiration, demonstrating that hard work, dedication, and artistic integrity can lead to immense success and acclaim.

Fueling Further Innovation: Each recognition motivates her to continue pushing boundaries, exploring new genres, and using her voice to advocate for important causes.

A Vibrant Portrait of Enduring Legacy:

Taylor Swift's journey of accolades is far from over. Each recognition paints a brushstroke on a vibrant portrait of an artist who constantly evolves, inspires, and uses her platform to make a difference. This ongoing pursuit of excellence, coupled with her genuine connection with fans, ensures that her legacy will continue to resonate for generations to come.

Chapter 9: Taylor's Version and All Too Well

Taylor Swift's artistic journey has become a captivating saga, where reclaiming control of her music and weaving it into cinematic narratives paints a vibrant picture of resilience, creativity, and authenticity. This tapestry is woven with diverse threads – legal battles, artistic visions, enthusiastic fanfare, and thoughtful critique.

Motivations and Challenges: The spark of reclamation ignited with the 2019 acquisition of Big Machine Records, leaving her first six albums' masters out of her control. Frustration at this loss of artistic agency fueled her to re-record these albums – "Taylor's Versions" – not just claiming ownership, but subtly weaving in "Easter eggs" for fans, a playful defiance against past limitations.

Adaptation's Canvas: But music was just the first act. Driven by a desire to express her narrative on a new stage, she ventured into cinematic storytelling. From concept to screen, each project held challenges. "All Too Well: The

Short Film" demanded meticulous screenplay development, casting decisions that evoked her characters, and overcoming production limitations. The "Carolina" music video for "Where the Crawdads Sing" saw her navigate the complexities of collaborating with filmmakers.

Emotional Resonance: Throughout, Taylor's emotions resonated. The frustration of lost control fueled the re-recordings, the joy of reclaiming her art poured into the films. "All Too Well," a deeply personal song, became a poignant cinematic exploration of heartbreak, revealing vulnerability and artistic growth. Social media posts and interviews offered glimpses into her emotional journey, connecting with fans who saw their own struggles reflected.

Fanfare and Critique: The response has been multifaceted. "Taylor's Versions" topped charts, fueled by fan enthusiasm over her reclaimed ownership. The cinematic ventures garnered acclaim – "All Too Well: The Short Film" won critical awards, while "Carolina" praised her visual storytelling. However, not all responses were uncritical.

Some questioned the re-recordings' artistic necessity, while others debated the cinematic adaptations' effectiveness.

Impact and Legacy: Yet, the impact is undeniable. Taylor's actions empowered artists to fight for their rights, sparking industry-wide conversations about ownership. Her cinematic ventures showcased her diverse talents, expanding her artistic landscape. The fanfare and critique demonstrate her cultural influence, where even disagreements engage with her work deeply.

Painting the Picture: Imagine Taylor, her eyes blazing with determination, meticulously recreating "Love Story" in "Taylor's Version," infusing it with newfound maturity. Picture the haunting beauty of "All Too Well: The Short Film," capturing the nuances of heartbreak with cinematic mastery. Hear the roar of approval from fans chanting "Carolina" at concerts, echoing Taylor's triumphant reclaiming of her narrative. This is Taylor's journey – a testament to the enduring power of creative control, where music and narrative intertwine, leaving an indelible mark on her legacy and inspiring a generation.

This exploration merely scratches the surface of Taylor's multifaceted journey. Each project adds another layer, showcasing her evolution as an artist, businesswoman, and storyteller. As she continues to weave her narrative, one thing remains constant – Taylor Swift's commitment to artistic authenticity and control, leaving a legacy that resonates deeply with fans and challenges the status quo of the creative industry.

Chapter 10: The Future is Bright

- Exciting ventures on the horizon and Taylor's aspirations and ambitions.

Taylor Swift, the ever-evolving artist, continues to surprise and excite the world with her artistic endeavors. While details surrounding her future projects remain closely guarded, speculation runs rampant, fueled by her cryptic social media posts and ever-present innovation. Let's delve into the potential paths Taylor might be exploring, unraveling the whispers of her upcoming ventures and personal aspirations.

Musically Unbound:

"Taylor's Versions" Saga: Will she continue re-recording her albums, delving deeper into her early catalogue and perhaps even venturing into the "Speak Now" era? Could these re-recordings take on thematic or stylistic twists, further showcasing her artistic growth?

Genre Expansions: With her masterful exploration of pop, country, and alternative sounds, might Taylor venture into uncharted musical territories? Could she surprise fans with an electronic music collaboration, delve into the depths of indie-folk, or perhaps even experiment with orchestral arrangements?

Collaborative Masterpieces: Taylor's known for her powerful collaborations. Could we see her team up with international artists, explore unexpected genre pairings, or revisit past collaborators like The National or Bon Iver for even more magic?

Beyond the Stage:

Directing Dreams: Having dipped her toes into directing with "All Too Well: The Short Film," could Taylor helm a full-length feature film next? Perhaps a coming-of-age story, a historical drama, or even a music video collection showcasing her evolving directorial vision?

Acting Ambitions: With her captivating screen presence, might Taylor pursue acting roles beyond music videos? Could she land a starring role in a major motion picture, perhaps even one connected to her own music or songwriting journey?

Storytelling in New Forms: Taylor's known for weaving narratives through various mediums. Could she explore songwriting for musicals, penning novels or poetry collections, or even develop a graphic novel series further intertwining her music and visuals?

Aspirations Unveiled:

Creative Freedom: Above all, Taylor's future projects likely prioritize artistic freedom and creative control. Whether in music, film, or other ventures, she'll likely strive for projects that allow her to experiment, express herself authentically, and connect with audiences on deeper levels.

Building a Legacy: Beyond accolades, Taylor might aspire to leave an enduring legacy that empowers young artists and fosters creative ownership. Could she establish mentorship programs, advocate for artist rights, or even create platforms for diverse artistic expression?

Balancing Act: As her career expands, Taylor might seek a healthy balance between personal growth and public life.

Perhaps she'll prioritize time for self-reflection, dedicate more energy to philanthropic endeavors, or even explore new personal interests outside the spotlight.

Remember, these are just educated guesses, fueled by Taylor's past endeavors and artistic inclinations. The true beauty lies in the unknown, the anticipation of what her creative mind will unveil next. One thing is certain: Taylor Swift's journey is far from over, and her upcoming ventures hold the promise of exciting surprises, innovative explorations, and a continued evolution of her multifaceted artistry.

- Pearls of wisdom and enduring values, Commemorating her journey and extending support.

Taylor Swift's journey isn't just about chart-topping hits and sold-out stadiums; it's a captivating narrative woven with threads of wisdom and enduring values. These principles, echoing through her music and actions, inspire not just fans, but anyone navigating the complexities of life.

Pearls of Wisdom:

Integrity & Resilience: From reclaiming her music to navigating public scrutiny, Taylor embodies unwavering integrity. Facing challenges head-on, she teaches resilience, reminding us that growth often lies beyond setbacks.

Empathy & Vulnerability: Her lyrics weave tales of love, loss, and self-discovery, resonating with diverse experiences. This empathy fosters a sense of community, reminding us that connection transcends differences.

Storytelling & Authenticity: Taylor embraces storytelling, crafting narratives that capture the nuances of life. By embracing her genuine self, she encourages authenticity, inspiring others to find their own voices.

Fan Devotion & Impact:

Commemorating the Journey: Fans create elaborate fan projects, analyze lyrical details, and celebrate milestones, showcasing their dedication and deep understanding of her music.

Extending Support: From supporting her chosen charities to participating in global discussions about music ownership, fans translate their love into action, amplifying Taylor's impact beyond entertainment.

Personal Tributes: Countless covers, re-imaginations, and artistic interpretations of Taylor's music demonstrate how her work sparks personal journeys and creative expression.

Enduring Legacy:

Taylor's influence transcends fleeting trends. Her music provides a soundtrack for life's ups and downs, offering solace, sparking joy, and igniting conversations about important issues. Through her commitment to artistry, integrity, and storytelling, she inspires a generation to dream big, embrace their voices, and leave their own mark on the world.

Conclusion

Taylor Swift is more than just a singer-songwriter. She is a leader, a role model, a trailblazer. She is a force of nature, a voice of a generation, a legend in the making. She has left an indelible mark on the music landscape, and on the hearts and minds of millions of people around the world.

Taylor Swift has taught us many lessons in empowerment and resilience, through her music and her actions. She has taught us to be fearless, to embrace our individuality, to express ourselves authentically. She has taught us to be strong, to stand up for ourselves, to fight for what we believe in. She has taught us to be kind, to support each other, to spread love and positivity. She has taught us to be hopeful, to overcome challenges, to pursue our dreams.

Taylor Swift has inspired us to implement her sage advice in our own lives, in various ways. Some of us have followed her example and pursued our passions, whether it is music, art, writing, or anything else. Some of us have used her songs as a source of comfort, motivation, or empowerment, depending on our mood or situation. Some of us have joined her fandom, the Swifties, and found a community of friends and allies who share our love and admiration for her. Some of us have simply admired her from afar, and appreciated her talent and spirit.

Taylor Swift has made a lasting impact on both music and culture, and we are grateful for her enduring legacy. She has revolutionized the music industry, breaking records and barriers, creating masterpieces and milestones. She has influenced the culture, raising awareness and advocacy, sparking conversations and movements. She has touched our lives, making us laugh and cry, making us think and feel. She has given us a gift, a treasure, a wonder.

Taylor Swift is a musical phenomenon, a cultural icon, a human being. She is a star, a hero, a friend. She is Taylor Swift, and we love her.

Made in the USA
Middletown, DE
26 June 2024

56368785R00055